How I Would Help the World

⚘

HELEN KELLER

How I Would Help the World

HELEN KELLER

Introduction by Ray Silverman

SWEDENBORG FOUNDATION PRESS
WEST CHESTER, PENNSYLVANIA

Library of Congress Cataloging-in-Publication Data

Keller, Helen, 1880–1968.
How I would help the world / Helen Keller.
p. cm.
ISBN 978-0-87785-336-7 (alk. paper)

1. Swedenborg, Emanuel, 1688-1772. 2. Spirituality.
3. Keller, Helen, 1880-1968—Religion. I. Title.
BX8711.K45 2010
289'.4—dc22

2010042829

Cover and text design by Joanna V. Hill
Typesetting by Karen Connor

Manufactured in the United States of America

Swedenborg Foundation
320 North Church Street
West Chester, PA 19380
www.swedenborg.com

Contents

List of Illustrations

*All images appear courtesy of
the American Foundation for the Blind, Helen Keller Archives.*

PART ONE

Helen Keller: Seer of a New Civilization

by Ray Silverman

some new joy, some fresh token of love from distant friends, until in
the fullness of my glad heart, I cry: "Love is everything! And God is
Love!"

Helen Keller

Tuscumbia, Ala., Dec. 9th 1893

Helen Keller: Seer of a New Civilization

The only thing worse than being blind
is having sight but no vision.

*T*hese are the words of Helen Keller, the world-renowned champion for the blind and deaf, the noble crusader for human rights, and the inspiring author who offered hope, faith, and consolation to all who strive to rise above limitations. Stricken blind and deaf at an early age, her life became a luminous example of the triumph of spirit over matter, hope over despair, light over darkness.

When we consider the life of such an inspiring person, we may wonder how Helen Keller was able to overcome her limitations and become such a powerful force for good. What was the source of her inner strength, undaunted optimism, and noble aspiration? She was an inspiration to millions, and continues to be so today. But who inspired Helen?

In order to answer this question, we will take a careful look at the life and legacy of Helen Keller, the blind seer of a new civilization.

Helen Adams Keller was born in Tuscumbia, Alabama, on June 27, 1880. A happy and vivacious baby, this lovely little girl spent nineteen months growing up as any other child, enjoying the beauty of the world and the melodious sounds of nature. Then, in early February 1882, Helen contracted an illness that has never been clearly identified, but that many people believe was scarlet fever. The illness left her blind and deaf.

When she was twelve years old, Helen wrote these words about her illness and its momentous impact on her life:

In the cold, dreary month of February, when I
was nineteen months old, I had a serious illness.
I still have confused memories of that illness. My
mother sat beside my little bed and tried to soothe
my feverish moans, while in her heart she prayed:
"Father in heaven, spare my baby's life." But the
fever grew and flamed in my eyes, and for several
days my kind physician thought I would die.

But early one morning the fever left as mysteri-
ously as it had come, and I fell into a quiet sleep.
Then my parents knew I would live, and they were
very happy. They did not know for some time after
my recovery that the cruel fever had taken my
sight and hearing. . . . Soon even my childish voice
was stilled, because I had ceased to hear any sound.

For the rest of her life, Helen would remain blind,
deaf, and unable to speak clearly. However, she did not
let her triple handicap stop her from becoming one of
the world's greatest social reformers—nor did she let it

diminish her exuberant spirit. In the next sentence she writes, "But all was not lost! After all, sight and hearing are but two of the beautiful blessings which God had given me. The most precious, the most wonderful of his gifts was still mine. My mind remained clear and active."

She ends her essay on a triumphant note: "My life is full of happiness. Every day brings me some new joy, some fresh token of love from distant friends, until in the fullness of my glad heart, I cry, 'Love is everything! And God is Love!'"

Truly, Helen Keller has become one of humanity's greatest symbols of the triumph of the spirit over enormous obstacles.

OVERCOMING LIMITATIONS

Life in Helen's dark, silent world must have been difficult and discouraging. Helen confesses there were times when she grew weary of groping in the darkness: "No one knows—no one can know—the bitter denials of limitation better than I do. I am not deceived about my situation. It is not true that I am never sad or rebellious."

Helen, however, refused to complain about her situation or allow herself to be imprisoned by dark moods: "Truly I have looked into the heart of darkness," she writes, "and refused to yield to its paralyzing influence. But in spirit I am one of those who walk the morning." And in another place she writes, "One can never consent to creep, when one feels an impulse to soar."

Helen intuitively knew that there was a larger picture and that her handicaps could somehow serve a worthy purpose in God's greater plan. Therefore, she refused to indulge in self-pity:

> Long ago I determined not to complain. The mortally wounded must strive to live out their days for the sake of others. That is what religion is for—to keep the heart brave to fight it out to the end with a smiling face. This may not be a very lofty ambition, but it is a far cry from surrendering to fate.

But to get the better of fate, even to this extent,
one must have work and the solace of friendship,
and an unwavering faith in God's plan of good.

She deeply believed that her blindness was part of God's divine plan and that her struggles against limitations would be wondrously transmuted into the gift of hope for others. In this regard, she adds:

Limitations of all kinds are forms of chastening
to encourage self-development and true freedom.
They are tools put into our hands to hew away the
stone and flint that keep hidden our higher gifts.
They tear away the blindfold of indifference from
our eyes, and we behold the burdens others are
carrying, learning to help them by yielding to the
compassionate dictates of our hearts.

This is a powerful thought: our limitations can be useful. As long as we do not allow them to discourage us, or drive us into self-pity, they can awaken our compassion.

They can become a means through which we begin to see and feel the sufferings of others.

Helen believed this idea most keenly, sensing that her special calling was to play her part not only in reducing the suffering of others, but also in contributing to their happiness. "Instinctively," she writes, "I found my greatest satisfaction in working with men and women everywhere who ask not, 'Shall I labor among Christians or Jews or Buddhists?' but say rather, 'God, in thy wisdom help me to decrease the sorrows of thy children and increase their advantages and joys.'"

It was perhaps the idea of service—a compassionate service that transcends religious differences—that disposed Helen to be so enthusiastic about the teachings of a Swedish theologian named Emanuel Swedenborg, and especially his idea of a "church." She writes:

> By "church," he did not mean an ecclesiastical organization, but a spiritual fellowship of thoughtful men and women who spend their lives for a service

to mankind that outlasts them. He called it a civilization that was to be born of a healthy, universal religion—goodwill, mutual understanding, service from each to all, regardless of dogma or ritual.

Helen also asserts that it was Swedenborg's teachings, more than anything else, that helped her to understand, accept, and transcend her limitations: "Swedenborg's message has meant so much to me! It has given color and reality and unity to my thought of the life to come; it has exalted my ideas of love, truth and usefulness; it has been my strongest incitement to overcome limitations."

Who Was Swedenborg and What Was His Message?

Emanuel Swedenborg (1668–1772) was a Swedish scientist and philosopher who believed that the Lord was establishing a "New Church." More than a religious organization, the "New Church" that Swedenborg described is the emergence of a new religious spirit in the world, a spirit that enables people to discern the truth for themselves apart from church dogma or the superstitious beliefs of a bygone era. Swedenborg called it "true Christianity." And, Helen adds, "It was his mission to teach people to listen to the inward voice rather than to opinions and disputations."

Helen was especially impressed by Swedenborg's teaching that all people could be saved, regardless of their religious background. In her book *My Religion* (more recently published as *Light in My Darkness*) she writes:

> I had been told by narrow people that all who were not Christians would be punished, and naturally my soul revolted, since I knew of wonderful men who had lived and died for truth as they saw it in the pagan lands. But when I read Swedenborg's *Heaven and Hell,* I found that "Jesus" stands for Divine Good, good wrought into deeds, and "Christ" symbolizes Divine Truth, sending forth new thought, new life, and joy into the minds of

all people; therefore no one who believes in God and lives right is ever condemned.

Swedenborg's doctrinal teachings were revolutionary in his day, especially the idea that all people (not just Christians) could be saved. He also taught that heaven and hell are not rewards or punishments; rather, they are spiritual realities that correspond exactly to our inner states. In effect, we judge ourselves by the choices that we make. While Swedenborg returns to this idea often, Helen sums it up in a few words:

> Swedenborg shows that the state we enter after death is wrought of our own motives, thoughts, and deeds. . . . [Therefore] it is our own fault if we live and think ourselves out of heaven. But we go there every time we think a noble thought; and we stay there when it becomes our happiness to serve others.

This idea that people judge themselves is central to Helen's understanding of God and religion. She was

repelled by the idea of an angry, vengeful, judgmental God who could only be appeased by a blood atonement. Instead, she found great comfort in Swedenborg's description of an infinitely loving Father who could never be angry with his children, and could not even look at them with disapproval:

> The new thoughts about the unity of God that Swedenborg offered as a replacement for the old concepts are precious because they give one insight to distinguish between the real Deity and the repelling appearance that results from a wrong reading of the Word. The following extract from *True Christian Religion* shows how Swedenborg strove to supplant those unchristian concepts with a nobler faith: "It may be evident how delirious they are who think, still more they who believe, and yet more they who teach, that God can condemn anyone, curse anyone, cast anyone into hell, predestine anyone to eternal death, avenge injuries,

be angry, or punish. On the contrary, he is not able to turn away from anyone, or look at anyone with a stern countenance."

Helen understood and took to heart Swedenborg's teaching that this loving God is truly worshipped through a life of useful service. She writes, "Sick or well, blind or seeing, bound or free, we are here for a purpose, and however we are situated, we please God better with useful deeds than with many prayers or pious resignation. The temple or church is empty unless the good of life fills it."

Because Helen yearned to be useful to others, she sometimes regretted that she had so many physical limitations. But here, too, Swedenborg's teachings gave her hope: "The dearest of all consolations that Swedenborg's message brings to me," she said, "is that in the next world our narrow field of work shall grow limitlessly broad and luminous."

One of Swedenborg's most unique features is his approach to interpreting sacred scripture. To him, every word of the Bible is holy and divine. But in the same way that we distinguish between a person's body and the soul that it houses, he makes a distinction between the literal teachings of the Word and the deeper truths it contains. He devotes many volumes to examining the spiritual meaning of the Bible, sometimes verse by verse. This is how Helen explains it:

> Swedenborg set himself the task of separating the dross from the gold, the words of men from the Word of God. He had a genius for interpreting the sacred symbolism of the Bible similar to the genius of Joseph when he revealed the meaning of Pharaoh's dreams in the land of his captivity. The religious leaders of Swedenborg's time darkened counsel with many words without knowledge. While they were helpless before the curtains of God's shrine, Swedenborg drew them aside with subtle insight and revealed the Holy of Holies in all its glory.

Swedenborg's interpretation of the Bible resonated with what Helen knew to be true in her own soul:

> I was glad to discover that the City of God was not a stupid affair of glass streets and sapphire walls, but a systematic treasury of wise, helpful thoughts and noble influences. Gradually I came to see that I could use the Bible, which had so baffled me, as an instrument for digging out precious truths, just as I could use my hindered, halting body for the high behests of my spirit.

Finally, Helen was not at all deterred by one of Swedenborg's most startling claims—that the second coming of the Lord is not a literal, physical appearance in the sky. Rather, it is a spiritual occurrence that takes place *in an individual* when the Word is opened and the spiritual sense of scripture is understood. Helen had no doubt that Swedenborg's writings contained the doctrine of the Lord's second coming. She called it simply "a doctrine of right living and true thinking"—the New Jerusalem descending from God out of heaven. Moreover, it was Helen's belief that Swedenborg's Latin message was a revelation of the spiritual meaning contained within the Hebrew and Greek scriptures:

> Above the cross was placed the inscription, "Jesus of Nazareth, King of the Jews" (John 19:19), written in Hebrew, Greek and Latin. It foreshadowed the time when the Lord would satisfy longing souls with his likeness, revealing the hidden meanings of the Hebrew Word and the Greek New Testament, and giving the spiritual sense in Latin. In this language Swedenborg wrote, translating, as God taught him, the symbols of the Bible into principles of practical life for the use and happiness of humanity.

How Did Helen Encounter Swedenborg?

As we have seen, the visionary teachings of Emanuel Swedenborg were the source of Helen's inspiration. This was the message that she referred to as "my strongest

incitement to overcome limitations." Our next question, then, is "How did Swedenborg's message come into Helen's life?"

This is the story within the story, and it begins with none other than the world-famous engineer and inventor Alexander Graham Bell. Bell had a lifelong interest in seeking ways to assist the hearing impaired. His interest in the field first arose because his mother was deaf, but it deepened when he married a woman who also was deaf. As Bell's research on speaking and hearing continued, he stumbled upon the invention of the telephone, for which he was awarded the distinguished Volta prize of fifty thousand francs—equivalent to about $200,000 today.

In 1880 (the same year that Helen Keller was born) Bell used the prize money to establish the Volta Bureau in Washington, D.C., "for the increase and diffusion of knowledge about the deaf." He hired John Hitz to serve as the first superintendent of the bureau. At the time, Hitz was living in Washington, D.C., and serving as the consul general for Switzerland. He was also partially deaf, and an avid reader of Swedenborg's writings. We will return to this part of the story in a moment.

Meanwhile, in Tuscumbia, Alabama, Captain Arthur Keller and his wife Kate had been trying to raise Helen. Now six years old, Helen was completely deaf and blind, and—from their point of view—incorrigible. The Kellers did not understand that Helen's incorrigibility was an external manifestation of her frustrated attempts to communicate. Desperate, and not knowing what to do with their "unruly child," they searched for help and eventually were directed to consult with Alexander Graham Bell. In the summer of 1886, Bell agreed to an interview with Captain Keller and his daughter.

The interview took place in Washington, D.C., over dinner. During that interview Helen sat on Bell's lap, felt his long beard, and sensed, through his touch, his kindness. Years later, she would write, "I did not dream that interview would be the door through which I should pass from darkness into light." After the interview, Bell recommended that they obtain a tutor from the Perkins School for the Blind in Massachusetts. They did as Bell suggested, and on March 3, 1887, twenty-one-year-old Anne Sullivan arrived in Tuscumbia to serve as Helen's personal tutor.

The story of Anne Sullivan's work with Helen is well known. In fact, it has become legendary as the story "The Miracle Worker," in which a young educator (Anne Sullivan) helps a deaf-blind girl (Helen Keller) find language and meaning in life. Helen called it her "mental awakening."

HELEN'S SPIRITUAL AWAKENING

But the story does not end there. After a year in Alabama, it was decided that eight-year-old Helen should go to Boston so that she could continue her studies at the Perkins School for the Blind. Arrangements were made and Helen began her studies at Perkins under Anne's careful supervision. All was going well, and Helen's fame was spreading. In her third year of studies, when she was eleven years old, Helen composed a short story for the school's director, Michael Anagnos. She called the story "The Frost King," and sent it to him as a birthday present.

Anagnos was delighted with Helen's story and promptly arranged to have it published. The story became very popular and was picked up by other magazines. But a sharp-eyed reader noted that Helen's story had many similarities to a story written seventeen years earlier by Margaret Canby called "The Frost Fairies." The two stories were more than similar; in fact, whole sentences and paragraphs were almost identical. Much to her surprise and dismay, Helen was accused of plagiarism, and an unpleasant investigation followed.

It was a difficult time for Helen, who scarcely understood what was happening or why she was being accused. In looking back upon that experience, she writes:

> No child ever drank deeper of the cup of bitterness
> than I did. I had disgraced myself; I had brought

suspicion upon those I loved best. As I lay in my bed that night, I wept as I hope few children have wept. I felt so cold, I imagined I should die before morning, and the thought comforted me.

As the investigation continued, rumors spread about possible dishonesty and fraud. The rumors found their way to Washington, D.C., and to the offices of Alexander Graham Bell, who had been following Helen's development with great interest. Unwilling to believe the rumor, Bell asked the superintendent of his Volta Bureau, John Hitz, to go to Boston, visit the Perkins School for the Blind, and discover the truth of the matter. Bell had great faith in Helen and was convinced of her innocence. As he put it, "I feel that in this child I have seen more of the Divine than has been manifest in anyone I have ever met."

When John Hitz came to investigate, he soon found himself as impressed as Bell. And he discovered that Bell's perception was correct. It was determined that

Helen was a child genius with a miraculously retentive memory. Hitz noted that Helen was one of those rare individuals who could store up information subconsciously and retrieve it years later. And he further discovered that "The Frost Fairies" had been read to Helen (by means of the manual alphabet) when she was eight years old. It had remained in her subconscious memory bank, covered over by many other stories and experiences. This explanation helped to clear Helen of all charges, much to the relief of everyone concerned.

As the case was coming to its conclusion, Margaret Canby, the author of "The Frost Fairies," wrote to Anne Sullivan, providing a final touch of graciousness. In her letter she asked Anne to give Helen her warm love, and to tell her not to feel troubled about anything, for she had done nothing wrong. And she added that Helen had actually improved the story!

So ended the sad case of "The Frost King," and so began Helen's happy friendship with John Hitz—a friendship that would extend over the next sixteen years

and lead to what Helen called her "spiritual awakening."
Helen remembers their friendship in this way:

> He loved to take me out walking early in the morn-
> ing while the dew lay upon the grass and tree, and the
> air was joyous with birdsong. We wandered through
> still woods, fragrant meadows, past the picturesque
> stone walls of Wrentham, and always he brought
> me closer to beauty and the deep meaning of nature.
> As he talked, the great world shone for me in the
> beauty of immortality. . . . We would often pause that
> I might feel the swaying of the trees, the bending of
> the flowers, and the waving of the corn, and he would
> say, "The wind that puts all this life into nature is a
> marvelous symbol of the spirit of God."

Throughout their long friendship, Hitz introduced
Helen to the great thinkers of the world, and especially
to the religious teachings of Emanuel Swedenborg. In
her gratitude, Helen called Hitz her *Pflegevater*—"the
foster-father of my soul." And Hitz referred to Helen

as "*meine innigste geliebte Tochter Helene*"—my deeply beloved daughter, Helen.

The first of Swedenborg's books that Hitz shared with Helen was a braille copy of *Heaven and Hell*. She was fourteen years old at the time:

> He put into my hands a copy of Emanuel Swedenborg's *Heaven and Hell* in raised letters. He said he knew I would not understand much of it at first; but it was a fine exercise for my mind, and it would satisfy me with a likeness of God as lovable as the one in my heart.

Such a book would challenge anyone fresh out of childhood, but Helen treasured that gift. A few years later, as her understanding began to develop, she started to appreciate what she was reading more deeply:

> When I began *Heaven and Hell,* I was as little aware of the new joy coming into my life as I had been years before when I stood on the piazza steps awaiting my teacher. . . . My heart gave a joyous

bound. Here was a faith that emphasized what I felt so keenly—the separateness between soul and body, between the realm I could picture as a whole, and the chaos of fragmentary things and irrational contingencies that my limited senses met at every turn. I let myself go, as happy healthy youth will, and tried to puzzle out the long sentences and weighty words of the Swedish sage. . . .

The words "Love" and "Wisdom" seemed to caress my fingers from paragraph to paragraph and these two words released in me new forces to stimulate my somewhat indolent nature and urge me forward evermore.

I do not know whether I adopted the faith or the faith adopted me. I can only say that the heart of the young girl sitting with a big book of raised letters on her lap in the sublime sunshine was thrilled by a radiance and inexpressibly endearing voice.

Helen rejoiced that she had found a way to read the Word of God that resonated with what she already believed in her heart:

> I was not "religious" in the sense of practicing
> ritual, but happy, because I saw God altogether
> lovely, after the shadows cast upon his image by
> the harsh creeds or warring sects and religions.
> The Word of God, freed from the blots and stains
> of barbarous creeds, has been at once the joy and
> good of my life.

It is no wonder, then, that Helen felt profound gratitude for the spiritual treasure that John Hitz brought into her life. On August 18, 1904, when Helen was twenty-four years old, she wrote in a letter to him:

> I confess that sometimes my limitations weigh
> heavily upon me. I feel weary of groping, always
> groping along the darkened path that seems end-
> less. At such times the desire for the freedom and

the larger life of those around me is almost agonizing. But when I remember the truths you have brought within my reach, I am strong again and full of joy. I am no longer deaf and blind; for with my spirit I see the glory of the all-perfect that lies beyond the physical sight and hear the triumphant song of love which transcends the tumult of this world.

Four years later, in 1908, John Hitz died of a heart attack at the age of eighty. But he would live on in Helen's memory as the foster-father of her soul, the ministering angel who came to her during the darkest time in her life. The interview with Alexander Graham Bell many years before had indeed been the door through which Helen Keller passed "from darkness into light." However, it was not merely the light of a *mental* awakening through Anne Sullivan; it was also the light of a *spiritual* awakening through John Hitz and the inspired teachings of Emanuel Swedenborg.

Social Reformer

Helen had many admirers, but one of her greatest was the American author and humorist Mark Twain. Calling her "the wonder of the ages," Twain wrote:

> Helen Keller has been dumb, stone deaf, and stone blind, ever since she was a little baby a year-and-a-half old; and now . . . this miraculous creature, this wonder of the ages, passes the Harvard University examination in Latin, German, French history, *belles-lettres,* and such things, and does it brilliantly, too, not in a commonplace fashion. She doesn't know merely *things,* she is splendidly familiar with the *meanings* of them. When she writes an essay on a Shakespearian character, her English is fine and strong, her grasp of the subject is the grasp of one who *knows,* and her page is electric with light.

Twain has another intriguing comment about Helen. This time he compares her accomplishments to the accomplishments of Napoleon Bonaparte: "The two most interesting characters of the nineteenth century are Napoleon and Helen Keller. Napoleon tried to conquer the world by force and failed. Helen tried to conquer the world by power of mind—and succeeded."

While Twain's comment is delightful, it should be pointed out that Helen was not interested in conquering the world; she was interested in *helping* the world. In fact, this was the driving purpose of her entire life. She saw herself as a social reformer devoted to relieving human suffering. Comparing herself to an equally famous French leader, she writes:

> I feel like Joan of Arc at times. My whole being becomes uplifted. I, too, hear voices that say "Come," and I will follow no matter what the cost, no matter what the trials I am placed under. Jail, poverty, calumny—they matter not. Truly he has said, "Woe unto you that permit the least of mine to suffer."

Helen did indeed carry the banner of social reform to all, and she fought valiantly to raise consciousness about the plight of the handicapped. But Helen's social reform did not stop at combating preventable blindness. She took up many other causes as well; she campaigned for women's right to vote at a time when it was politically incorrect to do so; she became a powerful voice against social injustice; she spoke out boldly against racial prejudice; she decried corrupt politics, denounced business greed, and openly deplored the horrors of war.

And yet, she always returned to the needs of the blind and the deaf. On their behalf, she traveled the globe six times, and visited dignitaries in every land. She spoke often and passionately not only about the plight of the handicapped, but also about their potential. In her footsteps, hospitals and schools sprang up as people began to realize that much could be done and that every human life is precious.

Wherever she went, Helen Keller became an inspiration for others. Whether she spoke about being blind, deaf, or deprived in any way, she had a profound effect on those who heard her. In a speech to a group of deaf children in Australia, she said, "I know every step of the road you are taking. And I rejoice at your cheer and determination, because the obstacles you meet are many. And when you go out to meet life's struggles and adventures, you will raise a banner for the deaf who follow you."

HELEN'S DEEPER PURPOSE

Helen's words to those children give us a glimpse of her deeper mission and purpose. Even though she spent her life as a social reformer—campaigning tirelessly on behalf of the handicapped—she knew that the advent of a new, more spiritual civilization would take more than social reform. She wrote:

> Now I am as much up in arms against needless
> poverty and degrading influences as anyone else;
> but at the same time, I believe human experience
> teaches that if we cannot succeed in our pres-
> ent position, we could not succeed in any other.

Unless, like the lily, we can rise strong and pure above sordid surroundings, we would be moral weaklings in any situation. Unless we can help the world where we are, we could not help it if we were somewhere else. The most important issue is not the sort of environment we have, but the kind of thoughts we think every day, the kind of ideals we are following—in a word, the kind of men and women we really are.

This may explain why Helen believed she could most help the world by making Swedenborg's teachings accessible for others. In her introduction to Swedenborg's *True Christian Religion*, reproduced in this book, she was emphatic about this:

Were I but capable of interpreting to others one-half of the stimulating thoughts and noble sentiments that are buried in Swedenborg's writings, I should help them more than I am ever likely to in any other way. It would be such a joy to me if I might be the instrument of bringing Swedenborg to a world that is spiritually deaf and blind.

Helen believed that bringing Swedenborg's teachings to a world that is "spiritually deaf and blind" would be her greatest service. It would be her attempt to help people discover, as she had, the unlimited treasures she believed were stored up in the Word of God. In doing so, she would help to restore confidence in scripture as a divinely given revelation of God's will. And she would help people resist the "evils of unbelief" that shake their confidence in God's unfailing love and guidance.

Helen knew what it was like to have her faith shaken, and she understood the mental anguish that accompanies those dark nights of the soul. In one of the last letters she would ever write to John Hitz (just two months before his death), Helen recalls a time during her college years when her faith was challenged. She also recalls how the teachings of Emanuel Swedenborg helped her to disperse doubts and sustain faith during that dark time:

> I had pursued a college course and found that true education consists in the knowledge of one's ignorance—the perception of one's littleness. Many doubts on religious matters had pressed me hard. The Word of God, the Way, the Truth, and the Life had been presented to me in our study of the Bible as fallible, a mere product of erring human minds. I was saved from the evils of unbelief only by the precious remains of faith which I had gained as a child. I cannot tell you how much I cherish a certain book you put in my hands long ago, a book which gave me to receive God's unfailing testimony and this kept the seeds of faith in my heart safe. I refer to *Selections from the Writings of Emanuel Swedenborg.*

It becomes clear, then, that Helen understood the importance of faith—the kind of clear-eyed, rational faith that she believed could sustain people during times of doubt and uncertainty. "I do not want the peace that passeth understanding," she said. "I want the understanding that bringeth peace."

This is the kind of peace that Swedenborg's message brought to Helen; and it was the kind of peace she wanted to bring to others. She knew that educating the mind was not enough to attain that peace; nor could it be attained through the advance of science and technology apart from the development of the spirit. Because of this, she advocated an educational system that would do more than cultivate the intellect; it would also teach compassion, consideration, and empathy. Helen put it like this:

> It is pointed out, and Swedenborg says the same
> thing, that humanity, *unschooled in love and pity,* is
> worse than a beast. It is a hornless, tailless animal;
> it does not eat grass, but it wantonly destroys with
> its reckless power of thought. We invent more and
> more horrible weapons to kill and mar our broth-

ers and sisters in war; we mutilate helpless animals
for sport or for the changing whims of fashion;
and we have a passion for faultfinding and scandal
that rises beyond control. Many other evils are no
doubt traceable to human ignorance, but certainly
not these pernicious tendencies. Our deliverance
is not going to be through self-culture unaided by
right desires.

Again:

We know that the international troubles of our
time, the hostilities between peoples, the menace
of war, are largely due to mental concepts that can
be changed only by suggestion, persistence, train-
ing, and sheer devotion to humanity. Nations have
become so dependent one upon another for the
support of life that war is more than ever mad-
ness. Yet so-called educated people are incredulous
of social, political, and spiritual developments
they may live to see and share. The small group

of believers who know must struggle on, bearing steadfast witness to their truth in schools, courts, workshops, offices, and legislatures; and what are they but messengers in their way of Christ's second coming?

These are some of the reasons why Helen wanted to make Swedenborg's teachings better known and more accessible. She knew that social reform was important. But she also believed that a lack of spiritual vision was far more destructive than the loss of physical sight, and that the inability to hear the voice of God was far more devastating than the loss of physical hearing.

PEACE ON EARTH

It is my prayer that this little volume might help Helen fulfill her desire to bring comfort to her fellow human beings. May it provide hope that someday fear, bigotry, and violence will end. May it inspire confidence that some day hunger, hardship, and needless suffering will be eliminated. And may it offer assurance that the powerful influx of God's love and wisdom will prevail on earth—overcoming hatred with love, conquering darkness with light, and replacing human greed with the joy of useful service.

When that day dawns, Helen's vision of a new civilization will be fulfilled:

> There are two ways to look at destiny, one from below and the other from above. In one view, we are being pushed by irresistible forces, obsessed by the fear that war, ignorance, and poverty will never be abolished. But looking up to the clock of Truth, I see that man has been civilized only a few minutes, and I rest in the assurance that, out of the problems that disturb thinking minds and warm hearts, there shall break the morning star of universal peace.

PART TWO

How I Would Help THE World

by Helen Keller

"I bury my fingers in this great river of light that is higher than all the stars, deeper than the silence that enfolds me."

Chapter One

A GREAT RIVER *of* LIGHT

*S*ince I was sixteen years old, I have been a strong believer in the doctrines given to the world by Emanuel Swedenborg. It was his mission to teach men to listen to the inward voice rather than to opinions and disputations. After many years of reverent study of the Bible, I gratefully wonder if I am not more indebted to Swedenborg for the faith that turns my darkness to light than I have yet realized. I acknowledge my profound indebtedness to Emanuel Swedenborg for a richer interpretation of the Bible, a deeper understanding of the meaning of Christianity, and a precious sense of the divine presence in the world.

"There are three things which flow into our souls from the Lord. These three, which are felt as one, are love, wisdom, and use. Love and wisdom, however, are confined to affection and thought, which exist in the mind. They come into existence through useful service."
—True Christian Religion 744

I have many times tried to recall the feelings that led me to take Swedenborg's interpretation of Christianity rather than my father's; but I can find no satisfactory answer. It was with me as it was with Joseph Conrad, when an irresistible impulse urged him to go to sea. Like him, I took "a, so to speak, standing jump out of my associations" and traditions—and the rest is what I have grown to be.

The theological teachings of Swedenborg are in many long volumes. The summation, the universal theology, is found in his magnum opus, *True Christian Religion*. Yet his central doctrine is simple. It consists of three main ideas: God as divine love, God as divine wisdom, and God as power for use. These ideas come as waves from an ocean which floods every bay and harbor of life with new potency of will, of faith, and of effort. To our conception of God, the Word, and the Hereafter, which we have received on trust from ages of unproved faith, Swedenborg gives a new actuality, which is as startling, as thrilling as the angel-sung tidings of the Lord's birth. He

"All this shows how sensually people are thinking when they say that nature exists in its own right, how reliant they are on their physical senses and their darkness in matters of the spirit. They are thinking from the eye and are unable to think from the understanding. Thinking from the eye closes understanding, but thinking from understanding opens the eye."
—Divine Love and Wisdom 46

❧

brings fresh testimony to support our hope that the veil shall be drawn from unseeing eyes, that the dull ear shall be quickened, and dumb lips gladdened with speech.

There is among us a distressing indifference to all things of faith, and impatience at any effort to explain the laws of life in spiritual terms. The only really blind are those who will not see the truth—those who shut their eyes to the spiritual vision. For them alone, darkness is irrevocable. Those who explore the dark with love as a torch and trust as a guide find it good. Blind people who have eyes know that they live in a spiritual world inconceivably more wonderful than the material world that is veiled from them. The landscapes they behold never fade. The flowers they look upon are the immortal flowers which grow in God's garden. Swedenborg's message is like the rock smitten by Moses, yielding sweet streams of healing water, even an abundance of truths for those who hunger and thirst in their pilgrimage through an age of materialism and selfishness.

"Peace has in it confidence in the Lord, that he directs all things, and provides all things, and that he leads to a good end. When one is in this faith, one is in peace, fears nothing, has no anxiety about things to come, and is disquieted by nothing. A person comes into this state in proportion as one comes into love to the Lord."

—Secrets of Heaven 8455

The doctrines set forth by Swedenborg bring men by a wondrous way to God's city of light. I have walked through its sunlit ways of truth, I have drunk of its sweet waters of knowledge, and the eyes of my spirit have been opened, so that I know the joy of vision which conquers darkness and circles heaven. Of one thing I am sure; any effort is worthwhile that brings comfort to limited, struggling human beings in a dark, self-centered age; and Swedenborg's message has meant so much to me! It has given color and reality and unity to my thought of the life to come; it has exalted my ideas of love, truth, and usefulness; it has been my strongest incitement to overcome limitations.

The atmosphere Swedenborg creates absorbs me completely. His slightest phrase is significant to me. There is an exquisitely quietening and soothing power in the thoughts of Swedenborg for people of my temperament. I wish I might be able to radiate the spiritual illumination that came to me when I read with my own

"Since life and love
are one and the same,
it follows that the Lord,
being life itself,
is love itself."
—Divine Love and Wisdom 4

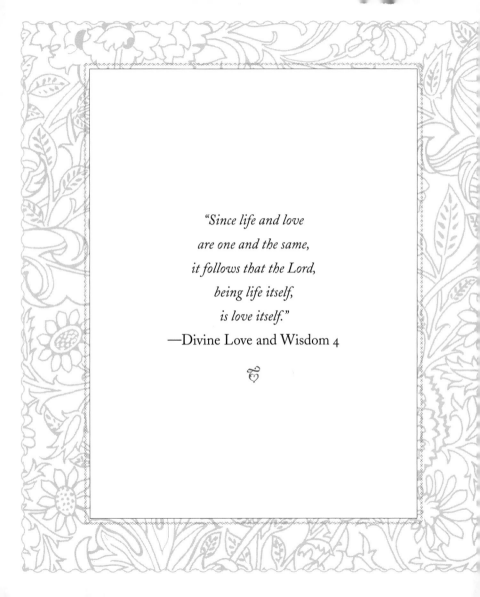

fingers *Heaven and Hell*. All the days of my life since have "proved the doctrine" and found it true.

If people would only begin to read Swedenborg's books with at first a little patience, they would soon be reading them for pure joy. They would find much to be glad of in heaven and enough to show them that the soul is everywhere, and enough to prove that love and God are so closely allied that we cannot know much about one and miss the other.

His *Divine Love and Wisdom* is a fountain of life I am always happy to be near. I find in it a happy rest from the noisy insanity of the outer world with its many words of little meaning and actions of little worth. I bury my fingers in this great river of light that is higher than all stars, deeper than the silence that enfolds me. It alone is great, while all else is small, fragmentary.

"In the Bible, rightly read and interpreted, is the truest and noblest conception of God possible."

Chapter Two

A NOBLE CONCEPTION *of* GOD

*W*ere I but capable of interpreting to others one-half of the stimulating thoughts and noble sentiments that are buried in Swedenborg's writings, I should help them more than I am ever likely to in any other way. It would be such a joy to me if I might be the instrument of bringing Swedenborg to a world that is spiritually deaf and blind.

The conclusion forces itself upon the mind of one who patiently read his works through, that Swedenborg described a world which was as distinctly objective to him as the world we live in is to us. It is also a fact that that world presents a system of perfect order, and every part of it fits into every other part. The same laws are

*"All religion is of the life, and the
life of religion is to do that which is good. . . .
A person may be doing the very same things,
but either from God, or from self.
If a person does them from God, they are good;
if from self, they are not good."*

—Life 2, 9

shown to apply to the constitution of the spiritual realm, the interpretation of the Bible, and the mind of a man. If the reader believes in revelation, he will find convincing proofs of Swedenborg's teaching in the Bible itself.

Three characteristics of his philosophy are completeness, homogeneity, and the universal adaptability of its principles. As a leaf grows out of a twig, or as the body depends on the mind, so is any part of this system bound to any related part.

All through his writings, Swedenborg teaches that all true religion is of the life and that the life of religion is to do good. He also tells us that the Word—the Law of Life—has its fullness, its holiness, and its power in the sense of the letter and in our acts. Every parable, every correspondence in the Word demands our faithful performance of every service essential to the health, enlightenment, and liberation of mankind. This means that we must strive to fill the practicalities of the world with the Spirit. If we think this is impossible, how can we call

"It is frequently said in the Word that Jehovah 'destroys.' In the internal sense, however, it is meant that people destroy themselves, for Jehovah or the Lord destroys no one. . . . The angels, being in the internal sense, are so far from thinking that Jehovah destroys anyone that they cannot endure even the idea of such a thing; and therefore when these and other such things are read in the Word by a person, the sense of the letter is cast away as it were to the back, and at last passes into this: that evil itself is what destroys a person, and that the Lord destroys no one."

—Secrets of Heaven 2395

ourselves disciples of him who died upon the cross that we might all have life and have it more abundantly?

Theologians have always endeavored to grip in permanent form man's momentary impressions of God from the fleeting, changing aspects of his world. From this process of dogmatism have arisen many of the contradictions in the literal sense of the Bible, and misunderstandings of God's nature and his purpose. Swedenborg had a genius for interpreting the sacred symbolism of the Bible similar to the genius of Joseph when he revealed the meaning of Pharaoh's dreams in the land of his captivity. The theologians of his time darkened counsel with many words without knowledge. While they were helpless before the curtains of the Shrine, Swedenborg drew these aside with subtle insight, and revealed the Holy of Holies in all its glory. The beautiful truths of the Divine Humanity had become distorted, dissociated, dissected beyond recognition, and our Lord Himself was lost in deadly dialectics. Swedenborg brought together the scat-

"We may gather how important it is to have a right concept of God from the fact that this concept is the very core of the thinking of anyone who has a religion. All the elements of religion and of worship focus on God; and since God is involved in every element of religion and worship, whether general or particular, unless there is a right concept of God there can be no communication with heaven."

—Divine Love and Wisdom 13

tered and broken parts, gave them normal shape and meaning, and thus established a "new communion with God in Christ."

Swedenborg was not a destroyer, but a divinely inspired interpreter. He was a prophet sent of God. The first and last thought throughout his writings is to show that in the Bible, rightly read and interpreted, is the truest and noblest conception of God possible.

Most human minds are so constituted that there is in them a secret chamber where theological subjects are stored, and their center is the idea of God. If the idea is false and cruel, all things that follow it by logical sequence partake of these qualities. For the highest is also the inmost, and it is the very essence of every belief and thought and institution derived from it. This essence, like a soul, forms into an image of itself everything it enters; and as it descends to the planes of daily life, it lays hold of the truths in the mind and infects them with its cruelty and error. Beliefs that set up ficti-

"Conjunction with an invisible God
is like a conjunction of the eye's vision
with the expanse of the universe, the limits
of which are invisible; it is also like vision in
mid-ocean, which reaches out into the air and
upon the sea, and is lost. Conjunction with
a visible God, on the other hand, is like behold-
ing a man in the air or on the sea spreading
forth his hands and inviting to his arms."
—True Christian Religion 787

tious excellencies and encourage devotional feelings that do not have for an object the good of mankind, become substitutes for a righteous, useful life. Such beliefs darken all morality. A supreme being is indeed worshiped with adulation, but in truth such empty ceremonies are most repulsive to the good and the wise.

A wandering idea of an invisible God, Swedenborg declares, "is not determined to anything; for this reason it ceases and perishes. The idea of God as a spirit, when a spirit is believed to be an ether or wind, is an empty idea; but the idea of God as Man is a just idea; for God is Divine Love and Divine Wisdom with every quality belonging to them, and the subject of these is man, and not ether or wind."

Guided by the light of the Divine Word, Swedenborg saw the oneness of God in person and essence, and Jesus Christ as God in the humanity that he assumed on earth, and the Holy Spirit as the infinite power for creating good and happiness. Jehovah wrought the most

"It is believed that God, the Creator of the universe, fathered a Son from eternity, who came down and took upon himself a human form. . . . This fiction is utterly exploded, like a meteorite in the atmosphere, when it is shown from the Word that it was Jehovah God himself who came down and became man and also was the Redeemer."

—True Christian Religion 82

stupendous act in earth's history as gently and unobtrusively as he pours his light upon mind and nature. One of the infallible tokens of divinity is its perfect quietness and self-effacement. When the Lord "finited" himself, as it were, and became a little child, there was no glory, except a light on the hills where the shepherds heard the angels sing, and a star in the far east. There was no sign of worldly magnificence or pomp. There was not even a man of perfect form and stature. Only a little babe lying in a manger. He was apparently just like any other child. His growth, mental and physical, was normal, and as we follow the story of his life, we find him a man with men, earning his daily bread as they did, walking with them along the seashore and by the hillside paths. Yet he was Immanuel, God with us. This truth is the center of all Christian doctrine, and unless one perceives it clearly, the Scriptures cannot be rationally understood. So one can joyously worship one God.

"All through Swedenborg's books shines an image of the eternal love that embraces every human being."

Chapter Three

A LOVE *that* EMBRACES ALL

The joy inspired by the concept of the Lord's Divine Humanity is like the sun with its threefold glory of warmth, light, and activity. It is like the satisfaction with which one beholds the happy balance of soul, mind, and body in a beautiful human being, or the perfect work of seed sprouting into blossom and the blossom yielding luscious fruit. How sane and easy and capable of fitting into the nature of all things such a concept is! Yet what prodigious effort it cost Swedenborg to plant it so that it could grow and flourish! The new thoughts about the unity of God which Swedenborg offered to replace the old are priceless because they give one insight to distinguish between the real Deity and the repelling

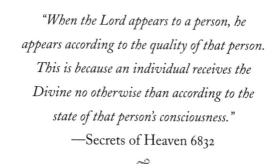

"When the Lord appears to a person, he appears according to the quality of that person. This is because an individual receives the Divine no otherwise than according to the state of that person's consciousness."

—Secrets of Heaven 6832

appearances with which a wrong reading of the Word and the anthropomorphic ideas of passion-driven men have invested him.

True Christian Religion shows how Swedenborg sought to elevate those unchristian concepts to something nobler. Hear him say:

> God is omnipotent, because he has all power from himself, and all others have power from him. His power and his Will are one, and because he wills nothing but what is good, therefore he can do nothing but what is good. In the spiritual world, no one can do anything contrary to his will; this they derive there from God whose power and will are one. God also is good itself; therefore, while he does good, he is in himself and cannot go out of himself. From this it is manifest that his omnipotence proceeds and operates within the sphere of the extension of good, which is infinite.

"In the universe and everything in it, God's omnipotence follows and works through the laws of its design. God is omnipotent, because he has all power from himself. All others have power from him. God's power and will are one. Because he wills nothing but what is good, he cannot do anything but what is good. . . . God is in fact goodness itself."
—True Christian Religion 56

And again:

It is a prevailing opinion at this day, that the omnipotence of God is like the absolute power of a king in the world who can at his pleasure do whatever he wills, absolve and condemn whom he pleases, make the guilty innocent, declare the faithless faithful, exalt the unworthy and undeserving above the worthy and deserving; nay, that he can under whatever pretext deprive his subjects of their goods, and sentence them to death; with other such things. From this absurd opinion, faith, and doctrine concerning the Divine Omnipotence as many falsities, fallacies, divisions, and chimeras have flowed into the church as there are subjects, divisions, and derivations of faith therein; and as many more may yet flow in as pitchers might be filled with water from a large lake, or as serpents that creep out of their holes and bask in the sunshine in the desert of Arabia. What need

"*The first essential of God's love is to love others outside of one's self. This is recognized in God's love for the whole human race. . . . The second essential of God's love is a desire to be one with others. . . . And the third essential of God's love is to render others blessed from himself. This is recognized in eternal life, which is the endless blessedness, happiness, and felicity that God gives to those who receive his love. For God is love itself.*"

—True Christian Religion 43

is there of more than two words—omnipotence and faith—and then to spread before the people conjectures, fables, and trifles, as many as occur to the senses of the body? For reason is banished from them both; and when reason is banished, in what does the thought of man excel the thought of a bird that flies over his head?

Such teachings lift one up to a mountain summit where the atmosphere is clear of hatred, and one can perceive that the nature of the Divine Being is love and wisdom and use, and he never changes in his attitude toward any one at any time. But all through Swedenborg's books shines an image of the eternal love that embraces every human being, and saves him from sinking into deeper sin.

Religion has been defined as the science of our relations to God and to our fellow men and what we owe to ourselves; and surely Christianity, rightly understood, is the science of love. When the Lord dwelt upon earth visible to mortals, he declared that on the two command-

"Because the Lord loves everyone, he wishes to do good to everyone. And doing good is service. Since the Lord does good or performs services indirectly through angels, and in the world through people, he gives those who faithfully perform services a love of service and its reward, which is inward blessedness, and this is everlasting happiness."
—True Christian Religion 736

ments, love to God and love to the neighbor, "hang all the law and the prophets." Yet for two thousand years so-called believers have repeated "God is love," without sensing the universe of truths contained in these three momentous words or their stimulating power.

Only when Swedenborg arose out of the cold age of logic-chopping called the eighteenth century, did love as a doctrine again shine forth as the center and life, the beauty and the preserver of all things. He interpreted the whole world of human experience as love and in terms of love—states of love—activities, powers, and functions of love—the constructive, preventive, and courage-stirring dictates of love. Moreover, the seer discovered that love is identical with the Divine itself, "that the Lord flows into the spirits of angels and men," that the material universe is God's love wrought into forms suitable to the uses of life, and that the Word of God, rightly understood, reveals the fullness and the wonders of his love toward all the children of men. Thus at last a faint ray, traveling

"We read in many passages that the Lord will come 'in the clouds of heaven,' but no one up to the present has known what the clouds of heaven mean. They have thought that he would appear in them in person. It has so far been unknown that the clouds of heaven mean the Word in its literal sense, and that glory and power, with which he is to come at that time, mean the spiritual sense of the Word. . . . The phrase 'clouds of heaven' means the Word in its natural sense, 'glory' the Word in its spiritual sense, and 'power' means the Lord's strength through the Word."

—True Christian Religion 776

through infinity from the Divine Soul, reached the mind of deaf, blind humanity, and lo! the Second Coming of the Lord was an accomplished fact.

Swedenborg's own mind expanded slowly to the higher light, and with deep suffering. The theological systems of his day were little more than controversies, and so full of long, drawn-out hairsplitting that they seemed like caverns in which one would easily get lost and never find one's way out again. Swedenborg had to define important key words such as truth, soul, will, state, and faith, and give new meanings to many other words so that he might translate more of spiritual thought into common language. For love he had to find a special vocabulary; indeed, it almost seemed as if he were himself learning a different language.

Out of his heart and out of heaven's heart he wrote, in *True Christian Religion*:

> The love whose joy is essentially good is like the
> heat of the sun, fructifying and operating on a fer-

*"The Lord's coming is not according
to the letter, that he is to appear again
in the world; but it is his presence in everyone;
and this takes place whenever the gospel is
preached and holy thoughts arise."*
—Secrets of Heaven 3900

tile soil, on fruit trees and fields of corn, and where it operates there is produced, as it were, a paradise, a garden of Jehovah, and a land of Canaan; and the charm of its truth is as the light of the sun in the time of spring, and as light flowing into a crystal vessel in which are beautiful flowers, from which as they open breathes forth a fragrant perfume.

Perhaps no one had ever endured such a pressure of soul against prison-bars of flesh as he did, and there was no reassuring nearness of equal intelligences to lighten his burden. He gave his life to learn, and what could he do with his colossal treasure of knowledge! He was naturally glad when more of light, more of opportunity was let into his difficult days; but I question whether he ever felt at home upon earth after his "illumination." Only such face-to-face knowledge gives reality to things, since it springs from life, and Swedenborg's living testimony will shed a slow but ever-increasing light upon the dark

"*The Divine itself, or Jehovah, is nothing else than mercy. In essence it is pure love towards the whole human race.*"
—Secrets of Heaven 2253

"hinterland" of our soul experience, and reinforce our groping efforts with the daring of immortal purpose.

Swedenborg's books are an inexhaustible wellspring of satisfaction to those who live the life of the mind. I plunge my hands into my large braille volumes containing his teachings, and withdraw them full of the secrets of the spiritual world.

Appendix: The Three Essentials
Compiled by Ray Silverman

*"There are three essentials of the Church:
an acknowledgment of the divinity of the Lord, an
acknowledgment of the holiness of the Word, and a
life of useful service."*—Divine Providence 259

Helen Keller and Emanuel Swedenborg both believed that there are three essentials of religion: a right idea of God, a right understanding of God's Word, and a life of useful service. This appendix compares the similarity of their views on this subject. The abbreviation (HK) stands for Helen Keller and (ES) stands for Emanuel Swedenborg.

A Right Idea of God

(HK) God appears small and undivine if a dull, perhaps bad person reads that God is angry with the wicked every day. But an individual of sense and heart sees that it is only an appearance and that we project onto God our own anger with each other and the punishment we have brought upon ourselves.

(ES) *Jehovah or the Lord appears to everyone according to his quality [or state of consciousness] thus as love and as the light of truth to those who are in good, but as an enemy and avenger to those who are in evil . . . The reason for this is that no one can see God otherwise than from such things as are in himself, so that he who is in hatred sees him from hatred, and he who is in unmercifulness sees him in unmercifulness. On the other hand, they who are in charity and mercy see him from, and thus in, charity and mercy.* (Secrets of Heaven 8819)

(HK) God is incapable even of sternness, and he tells his people this over and over again. As we penetrate into his Divine Word, putting aside one covering after another, we come closer to his true nature.

(ES) *It may be evident how delirious they are who think, still more they who believe, and yet more they who teach, that God can condemn anyone, curse anyone, cast anyone into hell, predestine the soul of anyone to eternal death, avenge injuries, be angry, or punish. On the contrary, he is not able to turn away from anyone, or look at anyone with a stern countenance.* (True Christian Religion 56)

(HK) The old view was most unworthy of the great God of all souls. He was supposed to have said nothing until Sinai. All nations except Israel were under his ban, and millions must have been swept into the abyss. Then his "beloved Son" interceded, and offered himself up as a sacrifice upon the cross for an otherwise doomed race; then the "Father" was propitiated, and canceled his sentence—but only for persons in whose behalf the "Son" spoke a good word! This old view was Swedenborg's arch enemy.

(ES) *Then a priest came forward and said: "God the Father in his anger against the human race damned it and shut it out from the sphere of his clemency, declaring all its members condemned and accursed, and consigning them to hell. He was willing for his Son to take that sentence on himself; the Son consented, and therefore came down, took human form, and allowed himself to be crucified. . . . Then the Father out of his love for the Son, and as the result of witnessing his suffering on the cross, was moved to pity, and decreed that he would forgive men, 'but only those to whom I impute your righteousness.'"*

On hearing this the angel kept silent for some time; he was so astonished. But eventually he broke silence and spoke as follows: "Can the Christian world have become so mad, and have abandoned sound reason for such ravings? . . . Is it not contrary to the Divine essence to change the laws of order established from eternity, which prescribe that each person should be judged by the life he leads?" (True Christian Religion 134)

(HK) Swedenborg confronted this giant with a new view that brought fresh hope and appreciation of the Bible. The God he followed is the God of all nations and all times. Swedenborg holds up many of the non-Christians of his day as examples of sincerity and well-doing that should put Christendom to shame, and lo! now it is they who are showing the most determined courage for the cause of brotherhood, while we devise more effective ways to kill one another in the next war.

(ES) *The Lord came into the world to conquer hell, open heaven, and save those who live according to his commandments. This is how it is to be understood, that, since all have been redeemed, they may be regenerated, and because regeneration and salvation make one, all may be saved.* (True Christian Religion 579)

(HK) All are born for heaven, as the seed is born to become a flower and the little thrush in the nest is intended to become a song-bird—if the laws of life are obeyed. In other words, all have been redeemed, and all can be regenerated, and it is our own fault if we live and think ourselves out of heaven. But we go there every time we think a noble thought; and we stay there when it has become our happiness to serve others.

(ES) *Every child, whether born within the church or outside of it, whether of pious parents or impious, is received when he dies by the Lord and trained up in heaven. . . . Everyone who thinks from reason can be sure that all are born for heaven and no one for hell.* (Heaven and Hell 329)

(HK) I had been told by narrow people that all who were not Christians would be punished, and naturally my soul revolted, since I knew of wonderful men who had lived and died for truth as they saw it in the pagan lands. But when I read Swedenborg's *Heaven and Hell*, I found that "Jesus" stands for Divine Good, good wrought into deeds, and "Christ" symbolizes Divine Truth, sending forth new thought, new life, and joy into the minds of all people; therefore no one who believes in God and lives right is ever condemned.

(ES) *That the deepest arcana lie concealed in the internal sense of the Word can be very plainly seen from the internal sense of the two names of our Lord, Jesus Christ. When these names are used, few have any other idea than that they are proper names and almost like the names of any other man, but more holy. The more learned indeed are aware that Jesus signifies Savior, and that Christ means Anointed; and from this they conceive some interior idea; but still these are not the things the angels in heaven perceive from the names in question. The things they perceive are still more divine. By the name "Jesus," when named by a man who is reading the Word, the angels perceive Divine Good; and by "Christ," Divine Truth; and by the two names, the divine marriage of good and truth, and of truth and good; thus the whole Divine in the heavenly marriage, which is heaven.* (Secrets of Heaven 3004)

A Right Understanding of God's Word

(HK) Swedenborg was not a destroyer but a divinely inspired interpreter. He was a prophet sent of God. His own message proclaims it more convincingly than any of his followers could. As we read his works, we are filled with recognition and delight. He did not make a new Bible, but he made the Bible all new.

(ES) *Although the style of the Word seems simple in the sense of the letter, it is such that nothing can ever be compared with it in excellence, since Divine Wisdom lies concealed not only in the meaning as a whole but also in each word.* (Heaven and Hell 310)

(HK) Swedenborg set himself the task of separating the dross from the gold, the words of men from the Word of God. He had a genius for interpreting the sacred symbolism of the Bible similar to the genius of Joseph when he revealed the meaning of Pharaoh's dreams in the land of his captivity. The religious leaders of Swedenborg's time darkened counsel with many words without knowledge. While they were helpless before the curtains of God's shrine, Swedenborg drew them aside with subtle insight and revealed the Holy of Holies in all its glory.

(ES) *The spiritual sense of the Word does not appear in the sense of the letter. Rather, it is within it, as the soul is in the body . . . The Divine itself is in the supreme sense of the Word. This is the most holy place, the Holy of Holies.* (Sacred Scripture 5)

(HK) Swedenborg develops a philosophy of Divine Revelation that is reasonable. He points out that, as in science, every revelation of new ideas from God must be suited to the states and the capacities of those who receive them. He undertakes to show that the literal statement of the Bible is an adaptation of Divine Truth to the minds of people who are very simple or sensuous or perverse. He demonstrates that there is a spiritual sense within the literal verse, suited to the higher intelligence of the angels who also read God's Word.

(ES) *The angels retain not even the least of an idea of any person, nor consequently of his name. What Abram is, what Isaac, and Jacob, they no longer know. They form an idea for themselves from the things which are represented and signified by them in the Word. Names and words are to them like dust, or like scales, which fall off when they enter heaven. Hence it may be seen that by the names in the Word nothing is signified except spiritual realities.* (Secrets of Heaven 1876)

(HK) What would a friend care about what I said to him if he took my words literally? Would I not appear to him mentally unbalanced if he thought I meant to say that the sun rises and sets, or the earth is flat, or that I do not live in the dark? It is the meaning my friend listens to, not the words or the appearances that they convey.

(ES) *All things of nature, and likewise of the human body, and also every single particular in them, correspond to spiritual things . . . And as Divine things present themselves in the world by correspondences, the Word has been written exclusively by means of them.* (Sacred Scripture 20)

(HK) The spiritual sense of the Bible deals with the soul exclusively—its needs and trials, its changes and renewals, not of times, places, and persons. When we read of mountains, rivers, lambs and doves, thunder and lightning, golden cities and precious stones, and the trees of life with healing leaves, we may know that they are exact symbols of the spiritual principles that lie back of them.

(ES) *Without a spiritual sense the Word as regards the letter is dead, for it is the same with the Word as it is with a person, who, as the Christian world knows, is internal as well as external. The external man if parted from the internal man is just a body and therefore dead . . . The same applies to the Word which as to the letter alone is like the body without a soul.* (Secrets of Heaven 3)

(HK) This rule of interpretation was employed by Swedenborg for twenty-seven years; and at the end of that time, he did not have to change or correct one biblical statement given in his first published work. He gives the same spiritual equivalent for the same natural object throughout the Bible, and the meanings fit wherever they are applied. I know; I have tried this key, and it fits. This is what Swedenborg calls the law of correspondences —analogies between the forms of nature and those of spirit.

(ES) *Every detail in the Word contains a spiritual sense, and therefore a divine holiness. This is because the Lord spoke purely in correspondences, and these were spoken from the Divine which was in him and was his. It is the same in all of the parables and in every expression which the Lord used; thus it is that the Lord said, "The words that I speak to you, they are spirit and they are life."* (True Christian Religion 199)

The Life of Useful Service

(HK) By focusing on their God-given talent, men and women who are becoming angels rise continually to nobler tasks; and each new state brings them an influx of new powers, which is what is meant by God's promise of "full measure, shaken down, pressed together, and running over." (Luke 6:38)

(ES) *Useful services are nothing other than works done for one's neighbor, country, church, and the Lord's kingdom. Regarded essentially, charity does not actually become charity until it passes into action and becomes a work; for loving someone but not doing anything good for him when the possibility exists is not really loving him. Doing good for him when the possibility exists, and doing it with all one's heart, is loving him; for then the actual deed or work contains all that constitutes charity towards him.* (Secrets of Heaven 6073)

(HK) In heaven we shall find the beauty and strength of men and women, selfless love between the sexes, the frolic of children, the joys of companionship, and the vital power of touch. So, in the light of Swedenborg's teachings, heavenly life is a truly human life, and there are all kinds of service—domestic, civil, social, and inspirational—to be performed and enjoyed.

(ES) *The whole of heaven is viewed by the Lord as a world of useful service, and each angel is an angel according to the service he renders. The pleasure in being useful carries him along, like a boat in a favoring current, bringing him into a state of eternal peace and the rest that comes with peace. This is what is meant by the words, "They shall have rest from their labors."* (Marriage Love 207)

(HK) Jesus told his disciples to go out into the world and to preach the Gospel of Service. He said that the world would not welcome them but this was not to trouble them. They were to be calm and to speak boldly. If a man took their cloaks, they were to give him their coats also, just to show that material things are of secondary importance.

(ES) *Jesus told his disciples to cast their net on the right side of the boat, and when they did so, they caught a great number of fish. And by this he meant they should teach the good of charity, and by doing so they would gather in people.* (Marriage Love 316)

(HK) Swedenborg says that "the perfection of man is the love of use," or service to others. Our halting attempts to act are mere stammering suggestions of the greatness of service that we intend. We will to do more than we can ever do, and it is what we will that is in essence ourselves. The dearest of all consolations that Swedenborg's message brings me is that in the next world our narrow field of work shall grow limitlessly broad and luminous.

(ES) *When a person is born, he comes first into the natural degree, and this grows in him by a continuous progression according to his accumulations of knowledge and the understanding he acquires by means of them, until it reaches the highest point of understanding called rationality. But still this does not result in the opening of the second degree, which we call spiritual. This degree is opened by a love of useful service in accord with one's intellectual attainments—but only by a spiritual love of useful service. This is a love for the neighbor.* (Divine Love and Wisdom 237)

(HK) Some churches realize that their people are leaving them; and, without understanding the cause, they try all manner of expedients to hold their flocks together. They say, "We are living in a materialistic age; we must give the people material attractions in the churches." As a result, we see preacher-actors, concerts, movies, bands, and frenzied acrobatics in some churches. Still, the exodus continues, the people murmur, and the light of faith grows dimmer in their hearts. What is the cause of this ever-increasing darkness in the tabernacles of God? Why are so many losing their belief in the livability of Christianity? While seeking the answers to these questions, I opened Swedenborg's *True Christian Religion,* and there I found an answer: "Where there is no good of life there is no longer a church." Where people cease to apply their beliefs to practical living there is no faith. Is that not what has happened to the Christian church?

(ES) *At the present time there is no longer a church, because there is no longer any religion in the Christian world. . . . Can there be any religion where it is taught that faith alone saves, and not faith together with charity? . . . Yet the whole of religion consists in doing good, and the whole of the church consists in the teaching of truths. . . . How glorious our lot would have been if we had welcomed these teachings!* (True Christian Religion 389)

(HK) Sick or well, blind or seeing, bound or free, we are here for a purpose, and however we are situated, we please God better with useful deeds than with many prayers or pious resignation. The temple or church is empty unless the good of life fills it. It is not the stone walls that make it small or large, but the brave souls' light shining around and in it. The altar is holy only when it represents the altar of our heart upon which we offer the only sacrifices ever commanded—the love that is stronger than hate and the faith that overcomes doubt.

(ES) *The life of charity consists in willing well and doing well to the neighbor, in acting in every work from justice and equity, from good and truth, and in like manner in every office; in a word, the life of charity consists in performing uses. Divine worship primarily consists in this life, but secondarily in [prayer and attending church]; therefore he who separates one from the other, that is, who lives the life of piety, and not at the same time the life of charity, does not worship God.* (New Jerusalem 124)

(HK) But we are not born again suddenly, as some people seem to think. It is a change that comes over us as we hope and aspire and persevere in the way of the Divine Commandments.

(ES) *It is an error of the present age to believe that the state of a person's life can be changed in a moment, so that from being wicked he can become good . . . and this by the immediate mercy of the Lord. . . . The mercy of the Lord, however, is not immediate, and a person cannot from being wicked become good in a moment . . . This can only be effected step by step as a person withdraws from evil and its delight, and enters into good and its delight.* (Divine Providence 279)

Further Reading

By Helen Keller

The Story of My Life, 1903

Optimism: An Essay, 1903

The World I Live In, 1908

Out of the Dark, 1913

My Religion, 1927

Midstream: My Later Life, 1927

Peace at Eventide, 1932

Helen Keller in Scotland, 1933

Helen Keller's Journal, 1938

Let Us Have Faith, 1941

Teacher: Anne Sullivan Macy, 1955

The Open Door, 1957

About Helen Keller's Life and Accomplishments

Herrmann, Dorothy. *Helen Keller: A Life*, 1998

Houston, Jean. *Public Like a Frog: Entering the Lives of Three Great Americans (Emily Dickinson, Thomas Jefferson, and Helen Keller)*, 1993.

Lash, Joseph. *Helen and Teacher*, 1980.

For Younger Readers

Dash, Joan. *The World at Her Fingertips*, 1991.

Obama, Barack. *Of Thee I Sing: A Letter to My Daughters*. 2010. (President Obama focuses on thirteen great Americans, including Abraham Lincoln, Albert Einstein, and Helen Keller.)

About Emanuel Swedenborg and the Teachings of the New Church

Henderson, Bruce. *Why Does God Let It Happen?* 2010

Keller, Helen. *Light in My Darkness*, 2000
  (revised and edited by Ray Silverman)

Rhodes, Peter. *Observing Spirit*, 2005

Rose, Jonathan. *Swedenborg's Garden of Theology*, 2010

Schnarr, Grant. *You Can Believe!* 2006

Silverman, Ray and Star. *Rise Above It*, 2005

Suzuki, D.T. *Swedenborg: Buddha of the North*, 1996

Taylor, Douglas. *Spirituality That Makes Sense*, 2000

The complete works of Emanuel Swedenborg, along with many other books about him and his teachings, are available through the Swedenborg Foundation, 320 North Church Street, West Chester, Pennsylvania, 19380, or visit **www.swedenborg.com**.

Acknowledgments
by Ray Silverman

This book has become a reality as a result of inspiration that came to a woman named Laurie Klein in a dream. Just before a meeting of women from various Swedenborgian denominations in July 2010, Laurie had a dream in which a large crowd insisted that we need to help Helen Keller help the world. She knew of an earlier work by that name that had been circulated as a booklet. At the women's meeting, Laurie told the dream and asked for help in taking this essay around the world.

In the opening paragraph of her essay, Helen writes, "I acknowledge my profound indebtedness to Emanuel Swedenborg for a richer interpretation of the Bible, a deeper understanding of the meaning of Christianity, and a precious sense of the divine presence in the world." I would say the same about my indebtedness to Helen.

I have long been drawn to her words, and have been moved deeply by her prose-poetry. In my opinion, she has fully succeeded in translating the "stimulating thoughts and noble sentiments that are buried in Swedenborg's writings" into words and phrases that simultaneously touch the mind and move the heart.

I am also grateful to Joanna Hill whose vision, determination, and encouragement have made this book possible. I would also like to thank Morgan Beard, David Brooks, my daughter Sasha, and especially my wife Star for much needed editing assistance. Helen once said, "It would be such a joy to me if I might be the instrument of bringing Swedenborg to a world that is spiritually deaf and blind." Similarly, I am tremendously grateful for this opportunity to bring Helen Keller's essay *How I Would Help the World* to a wider audience—perhaps to the whole world.